I0558678

From Village Roots of India & Teaching in United States

By

V.C.Patel

Prologue

I was brought up in an isolated village, named Dantali, in the rural Gujarat District of the state of Anand, India. The way of life in my rural district was based on agriculture and farming. There was little to be had, and dreams were likely to have roots in the earth. I lost my father when I was at the tender age of merely eight years old. Though my childhood was heavily marked with community and culture. My father's non-presence was a gap, and I was left with the responsibility of our home. Everything should be managed by the strong shoulders of my mother. Her unpremeditated fortitude and sacrifices were the foundation of my will to overcome adversity through education.

I held on to learning despite the financial hardships and troubles, social demands, and the seclusion of rural living. I started teaching in the small classes of Dantali, where I also read books under a flickering lamp. Through persistence, I got myself in the crowded classrooms of Indore, a city that widened my horizons. But still, my desire was greater. Venturing oceans, I landed in the United States, and I became a professor, and spread the word that had been my salvation. This book tracks that journey, starting from the farmlands of Gujarat to the academic halls of USA through grit, family backing and strong doggedness in education. It is a miracle of

i

holding back and surviving together with the power of dreams and the love of the mother who held me through all the obstacles of life.

Dedication

This book is dedicated to my mother because she has had to struggle alone and take the responsibility of raising our family after the death of my father. It all happened because her sacrifices, strength and support provided me with an opportunity to learn and lead a better life.

I also dedicate this work to my family; my wife and my children who have been with me during tough times of relocating to a new country and starting fresh life in the United States. My journey has been supported and nurtured by family's love and support.

Acknowledgement

I would like to thank my family, as they have always been my pillar to lean on. This has been facilitated by the sacrifices my mother made, the patience of my wife as well as the support of my children. The teachers and mentors in India, primarily Principal Wani, who helped me in educational and student years and influenced teaching practices are linked to my personal development as well. Finally, I can say that I am grateful to the colleagues and students in the United States who provided me the chance to pursue my professional life in the educational domain to nourish my skills further.

Table of Contents

Chapter 1: Early Life in Dantali

Introduction to the village and community of Dantali, District Anand of India

I was born in the small, rural town of Dantali, in Gujarat's Anand District, India, on July 20, 1940. Dantali was a town that was away from urban towns and cities, and remoteness characterized the simple but intimate nature of life. The village was a peaceful, rural community where nature cycles and farming tasks governed daily life. Everyone in Dantali was involved in farming and there was a feeling of togetherness among villagers. Farms were scattered all over, where crops were cultivated to give to the families who are residing there. Agriculture was not a career, rather it was a way of life that brought people together into a shared reliance on nature.

The social system in Dantali was extremely traditional with having a lifestyle in a community and family based. Everyone knew one another, and there was a certain understanding that held the villagers together. While peaceful, however, the village was in most ways isolated from the outside world. It lacked modern comforts such as sophisticated infrastructural facilities, schools, and other amenities. For a young boy like

1

me, the village was a playground and a school, but with minimal scope for growth and progress.

In this environment, family was a central feature in all walks of life. My own family, like most families, lived in a small homestead and owned small farms that sustained our basic livelihood. We kept cows for milk and engaged in other farming pursuits that sustained us and provided basic necessities. Life was not simple during my tender years. There were challenges that were a feature of country life, and yet the community assisted people who support each other in difficult times.

Family structure with Life Journey on a farm and the impact of losing father at a young age

My childhood was, like most in my village, built on traditional principles and values. I was raised with my mother, father and siblings. Tragedy befell me when I was just eight years old. My father died early in my life, and this experience would have a lasting influence on my life and future facets. My father's death meant that my mother was left to take on both the role of carer and bread earner in my family.

At a young age, I was not fully aware of how serious what had happened was. Losing a parent was something that was difficult for me to cope with, given that I was so young and didn't fully know what losing a father was all about. My mother was very tough and resilient woman. She took on the enormous responsibility for caring for us in my father's absence. She ensures that we were physically and emotionally cared for. Her dedication to all my siblings shaped my lifestyle and developed in me a sense of grit and perseverance that would serve to carry me through tough times later in my life.

Growing up on a farm in Dantali, I was no stranger to hard work. We struggled on the land with limited resources. Farming was not just an economic necessity, rather it was a lifestyle that taught me to respect hard work and responsibility during my early age. From seeding crops to taking care of cows, there was always something to do on the farm. These tasks, tiring as they were rewarding and impart a feeling of self-confidence in me.

In spite of all the hardships in life in a village, it also instilled in me a sense of community. We were not alone. We were part of a larger farming community in which neighbors helped each other with harvesting crops or caring for livestock. When times were tough, the bonds of mutual aid between villagers were invaluable.

Losing my father at an early age was a turning point in my life. Even though, I was too young to realize the magnitude of his death, it impacted my psychological and emotional development in a lasting way. At his death, I was compelled to grow up early, helping my mother in any way where I could. After losing a father meant that my mother was to be my pillar in life, and her dedication to raise us without any male presence in the family is something that I have always respected.

My mother's strength and resilience in difficult times was a guiding presence in my respective life. I learned that although my father's absence was a void, my mother's love, advice, and encouragement made me a person who I am today. Her persistent striving to give my siblings and me a future that shaped my own dedication towards educational field with diligence.

Losing my father also shaped my understanding of the world. I was taught from childhood that life is unpredictable and we have to learn to confront challenges that are head-on us. Despite this childhood trauma, my determination to thrive and to move from my past childhood strengthened me from inside. My mother showed me that life was not all about survival but about thriving in spite of what we went through.

Challenges of Early Education in India

Lack of education, or more specifically a lack of access to education, was one of the major issues I was raised with in Dantali. Access to education was rare in those days, and especially for children in villages like my own in Gujrat, India. We only had a small school in my village, and only availability of classes until fifth grade. The school was simple, with few resources and severe teacher shortages. It was not uncommon for children to learn subject material with no instructor. And textbooks were few and not having a proper guidance and mentorship.

Despite all these limitations, I completed my elementary school in my native village school from first to fifth standard. After completing this level, I understood that to continue my studies further, I would have to leave Dantali and go to school in the nearest town. This was an altering experience in my life. The nearest town, while still small, was wider in scope for schooling. It was there that I completed my sixth and seventh standard before going to a higher secondary school to complete my 10th standard, or matriculation by the time.

But this relocation to a town was not without difficulty. Traveling to town was not easy in any respect, and my mother found this relocation difficult to adjust to, especially having to

5

manage the farm on her own. Financial strain was a significant problem too. We made most of our livelihood from farming, and there was not always enough money to meet the school fees for attending school in town. My mother found a way to keep my school going in spite of economic strain.

The academic challenges that I was facing were not just economically in nature but emotional too. Transition from a small school in a village to schools in towns was a challenge to adjust to a new system. Being away from home and additional academic pressure was daunting to a certain degree. Still, my will to succeed and my desire to impress my mother kept encouraging me.

I completed my 10th class examination, which was a significant milestone in Indian education by the time. These were the examinations that ended school and were a precursor to university education. It was around this time that I moved to Indore, a large city in a different state, and proceeded to further studies in a university.

In Indore, I was confronted with a different set of problems. Living was costly, and I was compelled to stay in a hostel since the city was far from my native place. Although this was a strain on my pocket, I was determined to succeed in my life. My stay in Indore was also the beginning of a new experience in my life.

Growing up in Dantali, in the Anand district, was a blessing and a challenge. Life in a small village with a close-knit community and familial system inculcated in me good values that have remained with me throughout my life. However, losing my father at an early age and having difficulties accessing education in rural India were big challenges. However, I derived my strength from my mother's resilience and my own determination to succeed.

Education, which was difficult to achieve in rural areas, was always my priority, and it shaped my life trajectory. I have carried with me what was acquired in my childhood, and it has been a guiding principle throughout my life. From my childhood in a farming community in Dantali to becoming an educator and subsequently migrating to America, my life has been one of devotion and a love for education.

Chapter 2: Struggles and Triumphs of Youth

Responsibility of early marriage while in the tenth grade

As my mother had to single-handedly raise me, I had to face issues like many children in my age bracket could not even fathom. My journey was further intensified by an early marriage, which had a huge influence on my educational path and life choices.

At that time, marriage was not merely a personal commitment, but a social expectation as well. This was particularly so in my situation, with my elder brother also to be married. Family pressures cause me to get an early marriage while quite young in age. My cultural heritage and subtle pressures from my mother led me to marry when I was in the tenth standard. Though, I did not see my wife for three years due to studies. The weight of marriage was not a heavy burden in my life, and being very young in age was a determining factor.

It was a delicate and balancing act that early marriage brought in me. While being committed to studies, marriage introduced a sense of responsibility that many students in that age group were not saddled with. This was reflective of what society demanded in those days when societal expectations took precedence in determining what was to be in a person's life, even at the expense of individual desire and aspiration. To me, marriage's burden, even being a challenge, did not detract from educational aspiration. To me, education was the path forward and it was evident that success in studies would decide what lay ahead, not just for me, but for my new family as well.

The early marriage did not push me back as I have determination and resilience to characterize my future path. This would prove to be a mindset that would stand with me in good stead as I embarked on a demanding course of study while balancing my duties and being a husband, even from a distance.

Educational journey and overcoming financial and logistical challenges for higher education

Having lived in a rural village with few educational facilities from a very early age, my educational background was not defined as pursuing higher education. My school in the rural village provided schooling to grade five, and to study further, I had to travel to the nearest town. Nevertheless, despite these logistical challenges, I was determined to study even when resources were scarce.

By completing early education in a rural school, I proceeded to a nearby town to continue my studies, completing sixth and seventh grade. Schools in our local area were small then with very few resources and schooling was not always a priority in my family. It was a common trend to prioritize survival and farming activities at the expense of formal schooling. But with my mother having supported me in basic needs after losing my father, I push myself to pursue my dreams.

My next educational challenge was when I enrolled in a higher secondary school. It was a school that was a long distance from home, and it was therefore necessary for me to stay in a hostel. The long distance was a financial burden to me because it forced me to study further by my own expense. Having embarked on this new study chapter, I had to balance academic stress with being able to support myself to study further.

Education was not just about overcoming financial difficulties; it was about making sacrifices as a person. My determination to study in the face of many challenges brings resilience in me. The long-distance travel, financial difficulties, and stress of being away from home were constant challenges.

However, I persisted in knowing that education was the only way to improve myself and that of my household.

I then went to a university further away from home after high school. This was a new experience in my life and came with even more challenges in the city of Indore, India. However, these challenges did not deter me. I have continued to pursue studies with equal determination and commitment to achieving academic success. By 1970, I had a master's degree, a success not just in my life as a person, but one that also symbolized dedication to overcoming financial and logistical challenges that had always been present in my life.

It was a challenge to pursue a master's degree in India, especially by someone from a modest background. Academic life had to be balanced with part-time work to support myself. The high school teaching profession was a demanding one to balance with master's studies. The early morning classes and then the evening classes gave me very little time to rest, but I continued to adhere to such a demanding schedule until studies were complete. My experience highlights the importance of overcoming barriers that would otherwise discourage a student from fulfilling his or her educational dreams.

Power of self-discipline, Juggling studies and passion for teaching

During my academic life, my passion for teaching never diminished. It was not a career or a way to earn a living, it was a path that I have chosen by myself. From a young age, I had always been fascinated by the educational profession. It was due to this interest that I decided to pursue a career in teaching, even while pursuing my degrees.

While balancing studies for a master's degree with high school teaching, I possessed a strong work ethic and high degree of self-discipline. Having a clear goal in mind to be a distinguished professor, it was not merely about academic achievement, but also about being resilient to withstand the physical and mental stresses that involved in teaching and pursuing higher studies. My ability to efficiently utilize time and prioritize studies and work was a testament to commitment.

Self-discipline was key in my experience. Every day, there was a balancing act between study, instruction and ensuring that all obligations were met. Being without a car and being away from home and a career in teaching made each day even tougher. Most days were spent traveling by bike, with hours and hours of commutes to and from school to study late into the nights was a kind of passion in fulfilling my future dreams.

This grueling schedule required a tremendous amount of self-discipline, as it required unyielding focus and perseverance.

But what kept me motivated was always my passion for teaching. I loved imparting knowledge and guiding students, and that kept me moving in times of adversity. Being a teacher was not just a function of imparting knowledge; it was about shaping minds and instilling in them those same values of resilience and determination that had been instilled in me through my educational experience.

My desire to be a teacher was further fueled by the realization that education was a way to transform lives, not just mine, but those of students and their families. Throughout my professional career, classroom work was not just what it took to be a full-time teacher in Indore, India. In addition to being a full-time educator, I engaged in extra activities like giving online courses to date. This increase in professional activity was a direct result of self-control and consistent dedication to the educational profession.

My experience demonstrates that self-discipline has a central role in surmounting challenges arising from pursuing bachelor's and master's degrees, especially in the midst of financial and logistical challenges. It was such discipline that enabled me to balance responsibilities and leave space for passion in teaching. It dawned on me that in order to be

13

successful, I needed to have mastery of time, stay focused on goals, and be strong in times when everything was not as I planned for myself.

My life experience is a reflection of determination, responsibility and hard work. While being married at a tenth-grade level could have been a setback to most, but I had a strong desire to study, and my mother allowed me to ride out the storms of adolescence. The educational journey, marked with financial and practical difficulties, is a powerful reminder that with willpower and uphill battle, one can overcome with anything

My life testifies to the fact that personal challenges like early marriage, financial constraints, and balancing work and studies can be transformed into opportunities. My experience shows that with a love for teaching and education and a sense of discipline; one can be a change person. From what has happened to me during my early age, I can learn that success does not entail mere acquisition of qualifications. It entails while being dedicated to learning, being resilient in times of adversity, and being committed to spreading knowledge to others.

Chapter 3: Academic Interests and Professional Life

Completing Bachelor's and Master's Degrees

At that time my family had to go through some emotional and financial burdens, but my mother always been there for me. Despite that, she supported me to finish my education. At the same time, I also got married. Also, my elder brother's marriage was a timing consideration and I had not planned for my marriage to be the next day. I agreed because my mother felt that it was necessary to marry me at the same time. After three years, I met my wife when I was busy with college studies and staying in hostel far from home.

While I was at university, I had several things to manage. During my time in college, I had a part-time teaching job in a nearby high school. This was key to my survival as I had to make a living to be able to live within the city. This experience as a teacher so early on sparked a passion for education that I would carry my whole life. I loved teaching; I really enjoyed it, and I knew that education was not a career, it was my life's work.

When I had finished my matriculation, I moved to another university nearby. It was not feasible for me to go to the university every day as the university was about 12 to 14 miles away from home. It meant that I could not go and stay with my family, especially my mother who was managing the farming on her own. It was a difficult time for her, quite alone now to take care of the land and the household, and with no help from my elder brother, whose marriage was also going on at the same time.

At such a time, my mother was always there for me; she was always emotionally and financially strong. Even in the hardships, she urged me to pursue higher education. I was also married during this time. My marriage was planned because I was not immediately married, but it was a result of timing of my elder brother's marriage. I agreed with my mother to arrange my marriage around the same time. After three years, I met my wife, as I was busy with my college studies and living in a hostel away from home.

As a teacher, I also went to work on my master's. It was an immensely intense balancing work and studies. In the morning, I would go to college, teach in high school in the afternoon, and study in the evening. For several years, this became my life. I found it difficult, but in the process, I gained resilience, time management and the ability to work under pressure.

I had many things to do in my university years. During the time, I was completing my bachelor's degree, I took up a part time teaching job at a high school near my place. It was important for my survival because I had to earn an income to live in Indore City. This early teacher experience gave me a passion for education that I have had for the rest of my life. Teaching was an immense satisfaction for me and it became apparent that education was not just a career but my calling.

I was also working as a teacher while acquiring a master's degree. It was an intense experience to balance work and studies. I went to college in the morning, taught in the high school in the afternoon, and studied in the evenings. For several years this routine became my life. It was hard, but at the same time it helped me build my resilience, time management skills and an ability to work under pressure.

When I finished my graduation and master's degree, which was a big deal in my life. What followed was not only an academic achievement, but it was an affirmation of the work I had put in to maintain discipline in my life.

In 1970, I completed my master's degree, and it was a great moment in my life. This was not an academic achievement; it was a demonstration of how I persevered and had worked hard to manage my professional and academic commitments. I have gained a lot of knowledge in the subjects I studied as well as

17

the art of handling multiple responsibilities at this stage. Being a student and a teacher gave me a good foundation for my future career.

Teaching in High School and transition to university teaching

After my master's degree, I returned to the same high school where I began working part time to teach. Teaching in high school was very rewarding. I wasn't only able to teach my students but also to be a mentor and guide for them. During my years in pathology, I learnt the essence of patience, empathy and adaptability. As a teacher, I had different students with different learning paces and challenges, but it was my job to create a space for them to do well.

However, the real change in my educational journey occurred when I went to a higher secondary school that had an advanced level of education. This school, though, was the reason as to why I completed my eighth to tenth grades. This was a very crucial time in my life when I passed my first board exams, and it taught me how important hard work, discipline and dedication is. Passing the exams was a requirement from my studies and such learning gives the base of the future in my life.

In the classroom, I discovered that students liked an interactive format that can grab students' interest. In focusing on building a relationship with my students, I understood their strengths and weaknesses and taught my lessons based on their needs. So, I knew very well that education doesn't stop transferring knowledge but inspires students to think critically and independently. My experience in teaching in those early years framed my philosophy of education which would be a constant in my career.

When I was elected to be the school union head, it was one of the most significant experiences I have had as a high school teacher. The position was quite unusual because there was no formal election process, as the headmaster appointed me to the role. But it was valuable for me as I learned about leadership, responsibility and collaborative experience. I learned how to represent my fellow students, address their concerns and how to work with the school administration to improve the school environment.

After numerous years in high school teaching, I began teaching at the university level in the 1990s. This was a major step in my career progression as it gave me the opportunity to work at a higher level with the students. There were many differences between teaching at the university and in high school. At university level, the students were older, more independent and less focused on their time in school and more on their future careers. I was able to go deeper into academic subjects as I am a university lecturer, and I could really discuss more intellectually stimulating things with my students.

But that transition was not seamless. I had to adapt to a new teaching environment, learn how to communicate complex ideas to a group of students with diverse needs, and adjust to the different needs of university students. Meanwhile, I drew from my past high school experience of being adaptable and empathetic towards my students. The transition from university teaching was smoother as I had a good grounding as a high school teacher.

Experiences and Lessons Learned from mentors including Principal Wani

Over the course of my academic and teaching career, I had the good fortune to study with several mentors who had such a great impact on my journey. Principal Wani was one of my most important mentors in my life and he was also my math teacher during college. Principal Wani was a deeply knowledgeable person in mathematics and also an unrelenting man who worked for his students. He did not just impart academic knowledge but taught me how to be: how to live my life.

Principal Wani's teaching style was what made him stand out. He didn't just focus on making students memorize formulas or problems given to them but also made us think critically and understand the underlying concept behind them. Teaching taught me to love mathematics and further understand the subject. In addition, Principal Wani was available to his students both in an academic and personal manner.

Moreover, Principal Wani taught me the value of integrity, hard work and perseverance. He believed in his students' potential, and so did that give me the belief in myself and my abilities. The only thing he always used to stress was not to learn for exams, but to learn for life. His teachings really left an impression on me, and I still practice what he taught me to this day in my own teaching career.

During the course of my academic life, I am grateful and proud of everything that I achieved. My career in education has taught me that to get to where you want to be with perseverance, hard work and ultimately good mentors will get you there. From teaching in a small village school to helping students at the university level is something to acknowledge during my entire life. And the experiences and the lessons I've learned have been invaluable in terms of teaching, education, and mentorship. Principal Wani and my other mentors helped me many times in those challenges and showed me the direction of becoming the educator who I am today. Looking back on my career, it has been such a privilege to be involved in the educational journey of so many students and to be continually inspired by the power of education to transform lives.

Chapter 4: New Life Beginnings in the United States

Decision to move from India to America

I took a life-changing decision in 1990 that reshaped everything about my existence. I decided to depart from India when I relocated to the United States. I continue to carry both my professional dedication and the burden of my history as well as an unwavering optimism regarding tomorrow. The move out of India required a serious consideration because it emerged from professional needs and family circumstances. My son together with his family established themselves in America so I decided being near them became essential. The United States presented itself as the perfect location to chase my educational goals because it offered both professional advantages and abundant resources.

The process of reaching America involved multiple obstacles. During my early years I suffered enormous hardships because my father passed away when I was still young. His death created an enduring hurt which continued to affect me throughout my existence. My mother provided all necessary support and care throughout my life as my main caretaker while she worked to give me every opportunity for completing my education despite our family hardships. Through her constant backing, I succeeded in finishing my education and chose to immigrate to America.

Education became one of my constant interests throughout my childhood years. I developed an interest in teaching and learning from the very beginning of my primary school education through my years in high school. My destination throughout life has been to join the education system. The pursuit of my educational goals included earning degrees in physics and chemistry along with mathematics as my specialization field. My academic path developed through my intense love of learning and educating myself in India involved many obstacles. Financial limitations followed me throughout my academic journey, so I needed to monitor my expenses precisely to stay in line for the pursuit of higher education.

Unfamiliar Country and adjusting to new environment

My arrival in the United States brought absolute unfamiliarity with the atmosphere in addition to the environment and people there. Everything around me appeared completely unfamiliar since I stood in a strange place where I lacked any direction to understand my new life and its circumstances. I faced discomfort and unease because of my struggles with language and cultural differences and unfamiliar customs in the country. Beginnings in the United States brought forth feelings of being inferior because I lacked direction for my career and my travels. My first experiences revealed to me the extent of knowledge which I needed to acquire.

Stop and Go became my first employer after moving to America. The job offered me a chance to start constructing my new life in America despite its lack of glory. The night shift became my first workplace experience which completely differed from what I had known before. Every day around dawn the regular customer brought his usual cup of coffee to the shop for conversation. This daily exchange of words helped med to reduce my sense of isolation from the unknown surroundings of United States of America.

The difficult beginning did not stop me from pursuing my goal to become a professor. Success demanded that I handle both the cultural differences and academic pursuits of my teaching dreams.

Working as Professor at Lone Star College and part-time professor into progression to full-time faculty

I obtained employment at Lone Star College in Tomball Texas where I started teaching mathematics and physics as an adjunct professor. As my first role at Lone Star College, I took up an adjunct professorship that involved teaching both physics and mathematics on a part-time basis. The new career opportunity let me both transmit my education expertise to students and develop my teaching abilities. Teaching these subjects felt like a natural continuation of my physics and mathematics academic background, since I received degrees in both fields.

The first experiences of adjunct professorship included multiple obstacles to overcome. The part-time faculty role restricted my teaching hours, which required me to simultaneously manage my grocery store work duties. The compensation levels were meager, so I faced multiple and tough decisions about resources. Teaching brought great fulfillment even through the demanding circumstances I had faced. Various students with different backgrounds joined my classes where I learned as deeply as they learned from me. This educational experience provided me with both personal fulfillment and professional rekindling of my teaching career.

The adjunct professor position I held led to the chance of becoming a permanent faculty member at the institution. This major career achievement represented all the effort I had put into my career over the past years. I started my full-time faculty at Lone Star College during 1998 while maintaining my responsibilities for teaching both physics and mathematics to students. Additional responsibilities emerged and I received the chance to serve as department chair. As being in the Lab, I managed the operations of mathematics along with physics departments while leading faculty members and making sure all courses met the college standards. The new responsibilities from my role upgrades and brought increased responsibility and gave me satisfaction because I could contribute to the academic development program at the college.

Moving from part-time to full-time teaching became a dual success because it marked both professional advancement and self-achievement. My aspiration to teach students as a full-time instructor came true when I achieved this level. During this period, I gained the satisfaction of discovering where I belonged in this new nation after spending several years adapting to different surroundings of India.

My transition from India to the United States revealed both external and internal obstacles that I had to overcome. Relocating to a new country while leaving my family and every comfortable thing. I have to manage my mental difficulty and emotionally painful feelings. It took time for me to conquer my early feelings of inferiority after which I developed increased resilience in myself. My experience taught me to adjust to foreign customs, and I developed stronger belief in my ability to handle complex American situations.

I gained professional development from my duties as a professor. I developed skills for teaching students from different walks of life while mastering clear methods of presenting complex material to students at various knowledge levels. The experience allows me to create teaching methods which effectively interact with various student learning methods. The combined experience of instructing physics and mathematics classes brought extensive rewards which expanded my subject expertise beyond my expectations.

The financial hurdles along with cultural and professional barriers did not divert me from attainment of my goals. Becoming an educator and teaching students to improve their lives remained my central goal. The journey would prove challenging, but I stayed committed to continuing forward in my career path. The choice to relocate to America remains the best decision I have ever made to my present perspective.

The journey between India and America led me to transition from an unknown nation to my position at Lone Star

College as a full-time faculty. At the beginning of my journey, I took up employment at a grocery store because I felt uncertain about what to do and where to start in this unknown country and its people. I faced numerous obstacles, but my commitment to education together with perseverance pushed me forward to establish myself as a professional professor at Lone Star College.

I achieved my academic goals through teaching students who now achieve their goals because teaching is what my mother did to help me succeed. The migration to America was driven by my goal of working professionally, but I also wanted to find a fresh start while serving the community surrounding me. I feel great pride in the educational journey that led me through growth and learning toward transformation.

The students I teach keep inspiring me and I look forward to future learning possibilities which exist before me. The decision to migrate from India marked the beginning of my new life journey which I appreciate because it built the person who I am today.

Chapter 5: Road to Professional Attainment

Becoming a professor in the US

After a personal experience of experiencing my life before I arrived in the classrooms of the United States, having studied at my homeland and in India, I feel a deep amount of gratitude and achievement. And this chapter of my autobiography is an account of my career in teaching physics and mathematics. In addition, the awards I have won as the Best Professor of the Year, my unwilling adventures into the role of department chair, my experience in face-to-face as well as online instruction, and the priceless experience of being taught by my students and coworkers. The period of my life, which dates back to my entry into the US in 1979 and onward, was one full of challenges, successes and a strong sense of education that not only motivated my career but also shape my identity as an educator.

A lifelong interest in teaching at the United States inspired me to pursue the goal of becoming a professor in the United States. I began teaching way back in 1963 when I was a mere 18 years old and involved myself in the domain of physics and mathematics; a total of 16 years until 1979. I was not teaching just as a profession; it was my calling in India. I flourished in the participatory nature in which learning was interactive as opposed to monologic. It was not the jump in ambition that led me to the decision to move to the US but the continuation of what I knew best. Other activities such as business, research and administration did not appeal to me. I was expert in the delivery of knowledge, and I held that same zeal in the ocean. The US was the symbol of a hope, a hope to introduce my Indian-infused pedagogical style to a new audience.

I came there as an adjunct professor of physics, and mathematics into a community college. My initial actions in the classroom were nervous with fear. I was nervous and a bit frightened, as I did not know whether or not I would do in this new environment. Having a different nationality, my pronunciation was built under the influence of the British English and relevant to my Indian school system, which was quite different in comparison to the American one. I also feared that the students would not comprehend me or worse disown me. On the inside, I struggled with the self-sacrifice: "Will they be able to take in someone like me? Nevertheless, my co-workers would turn out to be my best friends. They were extremely great and assisted me with the specifics of the American academic system. They were warm and welcoming

31

knowing I was an immigrant, and they would always check up on me to be sure that I was alright. They were kind and made me not fear a lot and I fit well.

Juggling multiple roles

It is my style of teaching based on the Indian question-answer approach that really changed my experience. We did not depend on lectures only in India, we engaged the students. I would ask questions and measure their answers and expand on them, getting the participation of all. We would look at the faces of students based on predictive factors or misunderstanding and clarity or interest and change. Once a minor subject matter is done, I would use follow-up questions to have the students answer questions on their own instead of having to tell you what to tell. This was an interactive method that was more or less new to the US classrooms I visited where lectures frequently prevailed. My students took it in their stride to their satisfaction. They already in the elementary years liked such an approach, which seemed to them interesting and useful in terms of understanding complex ideas in physics and mathematics, such as quantum mechanics or differential equations.

My popularity grew rapidly. In a semester or two, students were competing to take up my sections. Classes would fill fast and too many students would be gathered in my office insisting on being allowed to participate. Even the senior students were telling the juniors, Take the Prof. Patels class and you will love it! I was very excited by this answer. It confirmed that my teaching style which was Indian also worked and succeeded in America. This began in the tutoring lab, where I tutored one-on-one classes, and this led to increased confidence. My approach was popular with students, and it was spread. I also no longer feared being rejected because of my accent since the feeling of appreciation replaced it. Indeed, even a few colleagues and students have praised my Indian speaking style, and they deemed it to be unique and adorable. This initial fame became the seed of a successful career, instructing the courses in the field of introduction to algebra to higher level astrophysics courses.

A high point of my career was getting the award of the best professor of the year. I was awarded these two or three times, a fact that showed the influence I had on my students. The prize was voted for by students and peers, and included a condition that once you received it you could not be nominated again within two or three years. This policy obtained a wider appreciation in the faculty. When I won the

33

first time it was overwhelming. I can vividly recall the ceremony, after the announcement of my name by the dean and applause reverberating in the auditorium. I have never felt it was more to me, that my ways were so far from a hit. Students traded glorifying recommendations about how I brought abstract concepts in physics (such as the laws of Newton or the field of electromagnetism) to life; using interactive discussion and making them fun. Problem-solving through questions in mathematics managed to remove the mystique of calculus and linear algebra. The fact that I have obtained this award several times provided me with the feeling that I am right into student-centered teaching. It was not only about the trophy; it was also the representation of trust and love my students showed towards me and this encouraged me to keep innovating.

Despite my focus on teaching, I couldn't entirely avoid administrative roles. I was put in interim department chair a few times, but not full-time. I never liked sitting at a desk scheduling and budgeting, but in the classroom. When the post was vacated by the sabbatical of a colleague, I was requested to fill it on a temporary basis. I received this reluctantly, because I had an obligation to be in support of the department. This was not easy to balance with teaching.

I managed the development of the curriculum, faculty meetings and distribution of resources to physics and mathematics programs as the chair. It took a lot of time, mixing administrative work and writing lectures on subjects such as relativity, or statistics. Problems were occasioned by the change of priorities administration that required diplomacy and paperwork, which did not resonate well with my desire to deal with students directly. Funny moments? Ok, one of them sticks out: in one faculty meeting, I bullied the word budget with my Indian accent where I said it was more of a bud-jet, and the room burst into good laughing. It was a breaking of ice, which made everyone remember that we are all the same. On a different occasion the scheduling went wrong and there was a clash between two classes in the same room. I was forced to make it up and it became a combined physics-math hour which students didn't hate. Such experiences taught me to be resilient, but I never came back to retelling not wanting to take on permanent chair positions and so stayed true to my calling.

My career changed and I gained something new through the development of education: I teach not only in the classroom but also online. Face-to-face classes were my strength, and I was able to read facial expressions and promote real-time discussions. Nothing could replace the power of a classroom full of students discussing a topic in the very life of a classroom, such as the concepts of vector calculus or thermodynamics. I adjusted, however, to online teaching, which appeared particularly after 2000, when such platforms as Blackboard became accessible (and later Zoom). Initially, it was daunting. What is your way of replicating the question-answer technique online? I was challenged with technical faults of bad internet, muted sound, or screen blackouts. One of the hilarious moments: we were attending an online physics lecture when my cat sat on the keyboard, and the classroom came into a frenzy, as equations were tossed around on the shared screen. Students laughed and it was an icebreaker.

Gradually I got good at it, with breakout rooms to ask groups questions and polls to get instant feedback. The online classes also broadened my horizons to enable me to educate a wide variety of students remotely, as well as working professionals. Online versus in-person implied twice as much physical preparations of demos in live classes, such as pendulum experiments, compared to simulations in virtual classes. The pandemic prompted such acceleration and made complete moves online. Student disengagement was among the struggles, but I responded with recorded sessions and interactive forums. In the end, this duality added value to my teaching, by playing traditional and modern.

Challenges and Rewards of Teaching

The experiences as a student and co-worker have been deep-seated ones in the course of my career. Among the students, I learnt the significance of being flexible. Their feedback educated me that my pronunciation should be perfected bit by bit and use American idioms without losing my identity. Another student revealed that I asked about his anxiety in math, so it was my approach, style of asking questions and answering that made him feel better, and this motivated me to make empathy a priority. The associates at work taught me to leverage teamwork and resource sharing on quantum computing or statistics modeling helped us as a department. They were also role models of the work-life balance, as they reminded me that I should not overcome them.

My Indian heritage helped in offering a variety of ideas such as applying Vedic mathematics in classes, which students enjoyed. Out of issues such as difficulties in pronunciation, I learnt the importance of being patient and humous in transforming what could have been an awkward situation to learning opportunities. The assistance of co-workers on my first steps made me feel a responsibility to do the same to novice staff members as a way of paying them back. Students trained to be modest; their silence in making me welcome to my classes managed to be so humbling, as well as reminding me that teaching is not about ego but empowerment. One heartfelt memory: a student of a related immigrant experience appreciated me as his role model, which means that representation does matter. These engagements enabled growth, which underlines the fact that education is two sided.

Reflectively, professional achievement came with hard work, creativity and human relations. The practice of teaching physics and mathematics did not simply involve equations and theories; it was a practice of awakening curiosity. Being recognized as a best professor made my work worthwhile, and acting as the chair though with limited terms made my world more open. This experience of walking between the real world and online space challenged my versatility with some successes and failures. The student and colleague insights on kindness, teamwork, power are the richest belongings to me. Looking back, I can proudly say that I have established a legacy of one question, one answer and multiple students at a time.

Chapter 6: Life Lessons and Philosophies

The Importance of Education

Education is the backbone of my life, the lighthouse that has drawn me out of the small pits of dirt in my village back at home in India into the broad horizons of the American dream in the United States. I was born to a poor family of farmers as V.C.Patel, and life in such a family taught me that survival was more than goals. Our village school ran as far as the fifth grade, and past that you had to walk three miles to visit the nearest town to get any knowledge. My colleagues, together with the rest of children in our community, have been leaving school at the end of primary school to work in the fields with their families.

The village was dependent on farming, planting, harvesting, and taking care of crops under the scorching sun. But I was different. The farm was never appealing to me; the farm seemed to me like a chain and not a calling. Rather, I sought and derived comfort and meaning in books and studying. This instinctive loathing of manual labor was no insurrection but an insurrection of silence; an insurrection of the aspiration to stamp his stamp on the world not with creation but with a creation of the intellect and not of the lineage. My out of

39

education became my savior, my weapon against the rut of poverty that was consuming so many of us around me.

This was a glimmer I caught at a young age through the efforts of my mother who is a tower of silent strength. Decisions were made together and there was sharing of resources in our joint family home where the grandparents, uncles, aunts and cousins resided under one roof. Our Indian society also held firm to the joint family system which underlines a focus on unity and supportiveness. It was not merely about sharing meals and sharing chores, it was a safety net that was made of love or sacrifice and shared dreams. When I was young, my father had died leaving me behind to my mother to face the burden.

However, in the extended family arrangement my uncles aided with the farm and the advice and emotional support of my grandparents. Such a collective spirit allowed me to think that my education was not an individual activity. It was a family investment. Although we were not rich, my mother wanted me to go on with my studies. Vehari, it will always be there, she would say, in the fields; knowledge, however, will carry you away where we could never, never dream of going. Her words called out the spirit of our family togetherness. One member's progress uplift everyone.

40

The three miles that I walk per day to school made me stronger in the higher secondary school. I finished my matriculation top in areas such as mathematics and physics which became my career in the future. Then the true test was college. The closest school was 12-15 miles, which was an unfeasible daily trip in our rural town in the times when scooters did not exist and trains were not reliably available. The only option was to remain in a hostel which was not cheap, accommodation and food that burdened the family budget. I was hesitant because I knew what my mother was going through, but she would not listen to it. The decision was endorsed in our joint family. My uncles contributed to bits, and my grandparents blessed the effort. Such solidarity meant that one more tragedy would become a victory together.

The role of family

Staying in the hostel helped to teach me to be independent but it also made me realize that I am emotionally weak. My homesickness was an issue as I struggled to master the weight of expectation, and I was a young man who lived in an insulated village. Night times when the suspicion came in, am I placing too much pressure on my family? Am I strong enough to succeed? These tender insecurities about me such as fibers

41

of worry and self-suspicion might have been unwoven by me. Family, however, and to my surprise, faith helped me. I was not much of a religious person during fasting and all the rituals were more of a tradition than of a belief. I found that there was a pragmatic overlap of faith and economy.

The hostel made a compromise: avoid preparing meals one day each week, by fasting, and thus economy. Not because of the prayer, but to relieve my mother, I selected Saturdays. The individual fasts were silent prayers of gratitude, and a means of overcoming my sense of guilt and putting it into discipline.

Practice over time has also enhanced my faith and likewise I have come to learn that spirituality is not necessarily about cosmetic moves but rather discovering inner peace even in a difficult world. The letters and weekend visits of my family supported this, as they are my lifeline, since I am vulnerable but not weak and the family makes me strong.

In the first year of college, my family activities interfered with my schooling in a very deep manner. My mother arranged marriages to my elder brother and me both at the same time as was traditional of two sisters of one family. I hesitated; marriage appeared as a way of forgetting my schoolwork. However, up in our collective family culture, such judgements were deferential to customs and reinforced alliances. I stipulated one condition: my wife would stay with her parents,

42

until I finished my degree. This trade off drew out the malleability in our family system and individual ambitions paralleled with communal responsibilities. Their help helped me to graduate with a bachelor's degree in physics, chemistry and mathematics.

After graduation, I relocated to a bigger city, where I got myself a part-time position as a helper teacher in a high school trying to get my master's degree in mathematics. The campus was massive since it accommodated the primary education sector to high degrees, but all of those were governed by the community.

My schedule was also tiring in the morning (between 8 and 10 AM) there were classes, then I taught between 12 and 5 PM in the neighboring building. This two-fold earned not only subsidized my education but also developed me as an educator. By the year 1989, I was promoted to be a lecturer of mathematics and physics teaching upper division students. Education had made me stop being a village boy who was not afraid of farming to become a respected professor. It ushered in an environment of stability, respect and self-dependence. However, all this would not shape up without the unchangeable support of the family unit. My mother's sacrifices, my siblings' encouragement, and the extended kin's contributions.

43

Emotional growth

I immigrated to the United States in 1989, at the age of about 40 or so to work at Lone Star College as an instructor. It was a leap of faith as it displaced the old joint family coziness to a nuclear family in a new country. New expectations in America were coming at a time when my emotional strength was also being tested. The culture shock, language peculiarities and the alienation of the extended family presented the moments of weakness and loneliness that ate my spirit away. In this case, religion was my comforter; day after day, I prayed and thought about the teachings of my mother, which helped me. I used the thoughts of our village home where family togetherness implied meeting storms. Back home phone calls helped in reducing the distance and reminded me that family support knows no borders.

The prevailing effect of education was on my children. Three children two sons and a daughter grew up in a combination of Indian values and American freedoms by my wife and me. We have established our values of joint family cohesion in visiting India and family get-togethers although we were a nuclear family in the US. I have stressed education as a must and my mother too. My oldest son went ahead and studied engineering as advanced by my passion for math. He went to a good university and graduated with honors now

44

working as a software engineer in Silicon Valley. One of the reasons behind his brilliant performance is that I have led a strict, disciplined life of balancing between work and study or how I did it during my hostel days.

Presently, I am a grandfather of five grandchildren, and the legacy of education is one that is increasingly happening. Growing up in the US my grandchildren can enjoy schools of the highest quality, which I always make them aware of their origin. We also preserve our family values by holding annual get-togethers in India where the relatives connect on the tales of what life in my village is like. My analytical inclination is reflected in one of my grandsons, whose major is computer science; one of my granddaughters is very artistic and combines her talents with her studies. Their achievements, doctoral projects, interns, self-betterment, all bear the marks of generations of learning focus. However, problems will come about: the digital generation is accompanied by such emotional careers as social media anxiety or school stress. It is in this case that I teach them to cope with weaknesses via family and faith.

I would advise basing talking to your parents, praying to have clarity, which is inspired by my fasting epiphany. It happened in one instance, when my grandson had a problem with bullying, our family led a counseling session followed by faith-centered discussions to convert his weakness into empathy and strength.

The joint family structure, though physically distant now, lives in our hearts. It educates that being together is not about being physically close but close in values. Family support entails compromising the dreams of each other as my mother did mine and my children. It builds resilience to emotional inadequacies, skepticism, fear and loneliness through a system of love. This is complemented by faith, which gives inner strength; my practical fasting became a spiritual one, which directs me through migrations and milestones.

Reflectively, education did not only mold occupations, it also molded character, which was strengthened by family and faith. Throughout village walks, to college halls, it raised me, my children and grandchildren to new levels never heard of before. With concrete hope that my autobiography will inspire you, I would like to write in one we shall be strong; in another we shall be wise; in another we shall be righteous; in another we shall be sacred.

Chapter 7: Reflecting on a Well-Lived Life

Cultural and societal shifts and the differences between Indian and American education system

Even sitting here in my American quiet at home and retired, with a full and productive teaching career, I often find my mind dashing back in time to the ways I have travelled. I am a man who lived between two worlds, which are India, where I was born and brought up and the United States where I have constructed a new life. It is my order to describe the tales that have made me who I am, what I have learned and the changes I have seen in cultures and societies. I would like to explore the cultural and the societal transformations I have undergone in this chapter and especially the significant differences in the education system of India and the USA. I am also going to consider the obstacles that have helped me get the most significant lessons, and how the difficulties made me develop as a person and become a professional.

Being raised in India in the middle of the 20th century, the society was highly traditional, community-based and hierarchical. Everything revolved around family and decisions were made by people collectively and respect given to the elderly and those in positions of authority were never questioned. Life in my village was based on basic rhythms: agriculture, celebrations and education as a way to escape unstable life. The community did stress on responsibility, karma, and interdependence. When I went to get my education, I did not do it in self-interest but with the aim of getting my family and helping in the upliftment of our community.

When I arrived in America at the end of the 20 th century, I entered a different universe. There was a cultural change that was swift and radical. Here, individualism reigns supremely. Individuals value their freedom of choice, self-expression, and creativity. In the USA, it is more of making your own way, occasionally at the cost of communal association. I recall that the first day in a busy American city the strangers hardly looked at me as compared to warm welcomes and questions at home. America is a diversity pot in the eyes of the society and everything in the world has its influences in America, creating the feeling of opportunity as well as isolation among the immigrant groups such as mine.

Among the largest cultural differences that I observed was the aspect of gender roles and familial dynamics. This was not the case in India where patriarchal structures were the order of things; women would be at home and men were breadwinners. In the USA though, I also witnessed women taking on careers with just as much vigor and families distributing responsibilities on a more equalized basis. This was a motivating factor, yet also I noticed the somber feeling that might be brought on by this sense of independence where you have limited extended families and are therefore left to depend more on yourself. The American society struggles with such social problems as racial equality and social mobility, which are different versions of caste and class conflict in India. Globalization has made Indian society change faster than in the past with urban young people now adopting Western dress style and technology which is easing some of the customs. Yet, the core values of resilience and spirituality persist.

Looking back today I can say how these changes have transformed me into being more adaptable, rather empathetic and open-minded person.

It was education that helped me in the passage between India and America, and it is amazing how the systems on the other side of the bridge are so unlike. When I was in school in India, the education system was strict, disciplined and authority based. The teachers were idolized Godlike figures. The curriculum stressed rote learning, memorization, and end of tests which dictated your future.

49

In India punishment was an established aspect of the process. I remember there were cases when a teacher could yell at a student because he/she was not paying attention or even apply physical punishment to light taps with a ruler or a harsh slap in case they made the same mistake. And this is the cultural kind of twist to it: parents fostered this. In case a child run home crying that he/she is being punished, the parents used to ask, "What have you not done? and they frequently co-operate with their reproach. Discipline was thought to make character and to guarantee success. No strict regulations were imposed against such approaches, it was society, and it was positioned on the concept of tough love that acclimates one to the harsh realities of life.

When I got to America and walked into my first college classroom as a professor, I was shocked. This system is student centered in that it lays great emphasis on critical thinking, creativeness, and expression of self rather than memorization. Classes involve the students in the interactive form of debate, in posing questions and even questioning professors. State of the art labs, libraries, and technology are plentiful.

Nevertheless, the most stunning surprise was the limits surrounding power. Early in my career co-workers cautioned me: "Do not touch the students, or you will get into trouble. There is no corporal punishment, no yelling and discipline is addressed by counseling, grades or administration. Forcing students to study? Unthinkable. Motivation is either intrinsic or extrinsic such as additional credit. This distinction is based on the wider values in society. Education in India is a family business, and one tends to be pressured to be a high achiever which is socially acceptable. Failure is socialized upon, and competition is profound. In the USA personal development and exploration of students in between majors, gap year, following passions are more of a thing. The American one is inclusive and accommodating various learning needs whereas the Indian is developing but is still struggling with inequality, particularly in the rural regions.

Lessons Learned from Challenges

Don't life's problems are the best teachers? They go to the point and bring our best out. I encountered number of them in my way and each of them taught invaluable lessons.

Immigration to America was the greatest. It was difficult to quit family, family traditions and a well-paid teaching position in India. With the cultural shock, adapted to new food, weather and social values, my determination was put to the test. But it made me flexible: change is not an enemy it is a chance to develop. I was taught to not fear the unknown and use homesickness as a driver to accomplish.

As a new entrant in the American education system, it was not easy to make a living in the profession. The differences in pronunciation made me embarrassed during lectures. And there were moments when my accent was misunderstood by students, and I was afraid that I did not fit in. Community members of India, at times, even did not believe that I was comfortable to teach there: You may not fit in. Nevertheless, I did not stop, and I continued to use American expressions and perfect my correction. This is what taught me perseverance: persistence breaks it through obstacles. The fact that I won the Best Professor award twice, confirmed that--the fact that my capabilities were confirmed by the peers and students.

Previously in India, teaching young meant a combination of work and study. There were real financial constraints; my family was not rich. This taught me to work with the little I have learnt to make the most of scarce resources, a lesson that helped me a lot in America.

However, as a retiree there are nuanced problems, such as the operation of a failing body or the absence of children. They tell me of gratitude: Of gratefulness after turbulent water. When I say bad times, I mean the best teachers. They also do learn about empathy-putting yourself in the place of others-and about humility, that success is a flash in the pan.

Altogether, challenges have made me realize that the discomfort is apparent growth. Avoiding is the stifling of the potential; it is taking them on the chin that constructs wisdom.

Personal growth and professional challenges

My personal development is overcome with the challenges of my career, each of which has made me a better person. Being a young Indian teacher, I developed as an amateur to a confident educator. Classroom management and patience were taught in the challenge of dealing with disobedient classes. On personal grounds, it created self-confidence. I knew that teaching was not only one of my jobs, but my calling.

This was enhanced by the immigration to America. Some of the professional issues included maneuvering bureaucracy to get visa and certifications, and cultural adjustment in education. I was not distracted by any other areas of my teaching. This mind concentration resulted in self-enrichment: discipline was the anchor of mine.

The barriers in pronunciation helped me focus better on communication, thereby becoming a better listener and

53

speaker. It has made professionally available to me a wide range of students and has diversified my view. Personally, it has helped me develop resilience and doubt that my community has reinforced my self-belief.

Nothing was achieved without awards and student criticism, yet nothing was achieved better than failure, such as the initial lectures when I felt out of place. They were instructing in reflection: the faster one analyses the mistakes the faster they get better.

Personal growth goes on in retirement with writing this autobiography because thoughts are organized, memories are revisited. My ethics were informed by professional issues: I can never compromise teaching ethics.

In the end, I was changed into a global citizen because of these experiences as a village boy. The time of growth does not stand in a straight line, but rather it is a mosaic of victories and tests. Now I have understood the importance of relationships, followed passions and mentored the younger immigrants back.

When I have finished this reflection, I can see an abundant life: full of experiences, intertwined with cultures and marked with endurance. To my future generation: changes, embrace changes, learn through challenges and grow unendingly. That is the spirit of the worthwhile adventure.

Chapter 8: Power of Persistence and Faith

Overcoming setbacks and journey through struggles

Life as I have learnt to know it is not a straight road with comforts and ease. It is a windy street we keep having to go through as we are always confronted by snags that challenge our inner being. These challenges have been both humbling and transformative to me, and that of V.C.Patel who was born in a poor village in India. This chapter is a retrospective of what it takes to go through a bad time in life and how to cope with the trials and tribulations and adapt to life in a new place such as the United States with its own pressures particularly with the multicultural life in teaching classrooms and an unforgiving family strength and a strong self-belief. These factors have been enforcers of my perseverance and belief to keep me going through the most difficult moments into times of silent success.

In retrospect, my life has been marked by a sequence of fights with each one of them making me what I am. The greatest challenges were at times early and were based on the cruelty of poverty and lack of opportunities in the rural India. By the time I finished high school, I was at a crossroad that could so easily have wrecked my dreams. My parents were not rich, my mother was a widow and with sheer determination had brought us up and could hardly afford a home. Our village of my childhood provided no colleges, no means of higher education. The closest was at the adjoining city, and I had to leave home and move to a hostel- a thought unthinkable in relation to our available funds. I recall the heaviness that accompanied that decision, and how many monsoons storm I felt like it was pressing on my head.

On the one hand, I was burning with the desire to know something; I dreamed of being educated, to get my family out of our situation. On the other I felt guilty when I thought of putting a strain on my mother with the hostel fees, books and expenses of daily life. How was it possible to have gone propelling my own ambitions, at the expense of her already frail resources?

This was the most difficult time and during this time, I heard a voice of doubt constantly in my ears. Sleepless nights were used to thinking of alternatives. Maybe, working as a street hawker in the village, farm, or giving up scholarship. But we started persisting, that silent work in us all. My mother O dear was my beam. She believed in me in a way that I was not able to see in myself sometimes despite my own struggles. Go, Vehari, she said, It is crying, her voice even. Education is your way out of this life. I will manage." She had trust in me, and it kindled my trust. I went to the city- Packing a small bag with her blessing, I went to the city and entered the college. The hostel was simple, the food bare but I was there.

The battles did not stop with arrival. The amounts of money added up to fast tuition, meals, and the price of a notebook all seemed like extravagance. I could not tolerate to request my mother to provide me with even more, so I created my own situation. I pursued chances of getting personal tutoring after the classes. It began in small steps: assisting younger students in math and science in order to receive some rupees. Word went round and I soon had a regular stream of pupils. It was tiring those evenings, working in low light, explaining to me what I had only learned myself that evening. I didn't have much time to relax, yet I learnt how to be a resilient person balancing studies with work.

Every dollar saved carried off the burden of my mother and supported by this fact, I felt that nothing was impossible in case of working hard. Towards the time of graduation, not only had I come out of the hurdle of financial problems, but I had also developed a background of self-sufficiency. This failure,

57

which was turning into a great danger, was a tale of perseverance.

Struggles in life did not end with education but they transformed. In India, professional life was also accompanied by its difficulties of establishing reliable jobs, coping with social norms and maintaining an extended family. At times when there were no job openings, where I could not get promotion because of prejudice. But each setback was a lesson. I also learned to be flexible, to find new competencies, and never to give up on the process. Persistence is not about walking without falling, it is about standing up and shaking it off and continuing onward.

Adjusting life in a new country and the pressures of teaching in a diverse environment of USA

This turmoil was maximum when I made a decision to relocate to the United States where there is a land of opportunities, a land that seemed miles apart to my village-like backgrounds. Coming to the city of Houston, Texas, in the late 20th century, I was thrown into a strange world. All was new--the spacious highways, the giant supermarkets, the sheer massiveness of everyday life. India, and in particular the villages, transportation consisted of bicycles or the rarely used

58

motorized bike depending on how much people could afford it. Autos were luxury and seen in cities. In this case, cars were a need in America, people had several cars in their families, and the streets would be deserted without the roar of engines. I clearly remember being on a street, and everyone zooming past, and I felt so alone. How are you supposed to get by here without driving? I wondered. There was less transport and any movement like employment, purchase of groceries or even social engagements had to be on wheels.

The challenge of driving came out as my instant adversary. I did not drive a car in India; I did not believe the ability was unnecessary. Now, it was essential. My son who settled down in the US earlier than I tried to teach me. He purchased a secondhand vehicle, and we went to classes. Yet the impediments were the barrier of culture. Respect to the aged is considered paramount in our Indian upbringing and children take their parents not to fault. My son would sidestep and hesitate to point out my errors, as late as it was, shift lanes, out of courtesy. The lessons became embarrassing; frustration was on both sides. I knew that this was not happening, the generation difference, which was increased by our traditions, could not allow any development.

I am not going to be beaten, and I took a risk. I made a temporary move to New Jersey here to live with my relatives, the son of my sister and his family. There, not beholden to a father-son sequence, I was able to study without sentimentality. I got a factory job to sustain myself and my first salary checks allowed me to pay a professional driving instructor. Such sessions were also tough: getting up early to train turns, get used to the traffic, learn to park. Errors were honestly and unhesitatingly corrected, and at no expense of my own. Three or four months later I took my driving exam and got my license. Coming back to Houston I was liberated. It made the car my passport to self-sufficient, and I was able to visit this new land on my own condition.

It was not only in driving that one was adjusted. The cultural shock was serious. In India community was close; neighbors were part of the family. Individualist reigned people in the US were polite but remote. There was a conflict of languages as my own English which was good had an accent that on occasion gave me a poor reception. Another challenge was food; spicy curries were replaced by unhealthy fast food before I knew how to make some of the known food.

Then the professional demands, especially in teaching, followed. My initial step in the education world in this country was not big. I needed work and one evening I went to a nearby college at about 7 PM. There was not much noise there--just a stuffing of ladies in the lab. I pleaded for any position. In the

60

evenings, 5-8 PM, they tutored students on math and science in library. With a foothold I accepted it eagerly.

The American education system was a great place to teach. Classrooms were filled with students from all corners of the world- Latin America, Asia, Africa, and Europe. Their backgrounds were in a most eclectic mix: some were first-generation immigrants as I was, others were native born with varying learning orientations. Strains strained by fitting into this mosaic. I needed to overcome cultural sensitivities of explaining the ideas in a manner that would make sense within cross-linguistic and cross-experiences. A student may understand algebra by reference to the farming world, another one by technology. Misinterpretations occurred; an epithet which landed in India went sour here, or a strictness which was construed as cruelty.

Even the academia was challenging. The process of education in India was rote based; in this case, it was focused on critical thinking and interaction. I was also subjected to inspection by supervisors to make sure that my ways were in accordance with standards. The tutoring hours were very exhausting, particularly when I had to couple it with family. But the strains sharpened my talents. I am taught about empathy, and how to modify lessons according to people. Gradually, I went a step higher and became a tutor, then tutor

61

turned into lecturing, and I enjoyed a variety of classrooms. The activities of students became mine. It was not easy to adjust but endurance made misfortunes to be strong.

Strength from family and belief in oneself

By all this what sustained me? Family and an unshakeable belief in myself. Their well-being of my sons, daughters and grandkids has always been my primary aim. Their joy is my North Star. Finances strained in a country where I lived in India was one of the thoughts that led me to tutoring gigs. During the process of driving vowels in the US, the realization that my independence was going to relieve them prompted me to keep on in the process.

The support of family was physically provided by my mother, as well as by my son at the beginning and the hospitality of family members in New Jersey. And also, it was emotional letters back home and calls that reminded me of roots. Belief was a factor as well; my Hinduism had taught me about karma and perseverance. Prayers focused on me at times of life lows.

But real power was inward. The first step to persistence is belief in oneself. I believed in my power to adjust, educate, get over. The thought of doubt filled me, and I remembered former wins at high school to college, village to America. It was this self-belief along with family that made disappointments steppingstones.

Reflectively, my experience highlights the importance of perseverance and belief. Struggles make us strong like rock and overcoming any obstacle that comes in my way. Adjustments make us fine and inner powers drive us on. I owe these lessons to life to my family; to my family, I am grateful. It is my hope that as I write this autobiography my story will inspire nothing is a dead end when taken with determination.

Chapter 9: Legacy and Next Generation

Thinking about the canvas of my life, I can say that the colors of the tapestry made by my family are the brightest. My grandchildren are in the center of this legacy because they are not only the continuation of our family but also the embodiment of happiness, sense of meaning, and renewal. Grandchildren are the jewels of the lives of grandparents in our society. They arrive, first of all, overwhelming all other priorities, with their innocent laughter and their unrestricted energy. They are all to me more than words can say, 100% more than my heart can hold. They are the walking personification of unconditional love, in which a grandparent will move mountains, give up comforts, and empty out their pocket with love without a second count. This is a sacred bond in our culture; a giving back cycle much like how we were given to by our own elders.

Grandchildren play a role in the life of their grandparent as it is multifaceted and significant. They illuminate the dark years and make the normal days into feasts of pleasure. I recall that the early part of my life was a storm of duties of a business to build, kids to raise, dealing with the difficulties of the migrant world and adjustment. However, when my grandchildren came, a new page was written, and it was one of innocent and untainted joy. They stand in between the past and the future and bring our traditions with them and imbue them with new visions. Grandchildren are perceived as the bearers of the family legacy in our Patel community. At our knees they get to know our stories, rituals and values so that the flame of our ancestry stays alive even to generations yet to come.

What actually makes this role great is the pride that they give us. It is not merely pride in the grandchildren because in their eyes, one can see the results of their lifelong working reflected. I may cite a fragment, which yet gladden my heart: It was one of those family reunions a few years ago when my eldest grand son, then only twelve years old, took to his feet to read a poem he had composed on our family immigration to our new abode.

The strength, industry and cohesion with which I had spent so many evenings with him in telling stories. When he was done the room rose up to applause, but it was how he looked at me, with a sense of gratitude and of determination, that swelled my chest with pride. In that moment I did not only observe a child, but a young man who represented the power of our line. He had absorbed what I had taught and had turned it into his own, and this showed that whatever we teach can be flowered in a most unexpected manner. It is at times like these that I remember how grandchildren are our moving legacy;

65

how they justify our difficult times and increase our delight in the good ones.

This sense of pride goes beyond personal anecdotes to what the grandchildren can do to keep the family together. And they unite us and heal us of any division with their childlike charisma. Given that extended families are the norm in our society, grandchildren are the unifying force, bringing together the grandparents, parents, and siblings into experiences. They also teach us to be patient, to revive our sense of wonder and even to stay young at heart. I even find myself have to play some games that I hadn't played in decades or read about new technologies simply to get connected to them. Their existence is a lesson that is not collecting but sharing love and knowledge.

Leaving the comfort of the family relationship, I address the concern of education in the new generation as one of the pillars by which I will stand in the future. Education in my life was not always easy; I had limited chances as a young man living in rural India and had to struggle through self-education and will power. I can now look out at my grandchildren and future generations and make it very clear to them that education is the door to potential and guaranteed success. It is not about what one learns but character, strength and a way to be independent.

Education is valuable because it transforms. It provides the young with the resources to operate in an ever-evolving world, as it encourages them to think critically and innovatively, as well as be compassionate. We believe that education is in our culture a holy obligation, something that must be used to commemorate our ancestors by overcoming the shackles.

I would like to convey the message that you should never give up as soon as you step into the process of learning. They have to be continuous; any interruption to education derails progress, just as a river which has been held up loses its strength. The only news I can give to the future generation is very basic and yet very fundamental: Be always in touch with your studies, however far the hurdles. Whether it is on higher degrees, vocational training or lifelong learning, perseverance transforms potential to success.

Look at the bigger picture: Educated people not only themselves but whole communities are raised. We have witnessed in our Patel family how education has helped us to forge ahead as a family out of humble origins into the international scene. This ethos helped my own children, and they are currently in schools which value not only academics but values as well. Discipline, horizons and equipping one with the uncertainties in life is what education brings about. Without it, the dreams would not be accomplished but with it, there would be no stairs to heaven. I encourage young people to listen to their parents' advice in this aspect because parental knowledge can normally guide us in achieving excellence in education. In fact, deferring the aged individuals is confounded with the learning achievement which all studying is built on.

However, schooling is not sufficient, family and faith in oneself are the keys. Family forms the foundation of our lives, which offers unequivocal support that drives the growth of the individual. The family strength was experienced in all milestones in my journey, such as the challenges of a tight financial situation to the joy at the victory. Our extended, well-knit family provided emotional support, wise counsel and a lifeline when it was time to pull on. Family power teaches us that we never stand alone; but it is a greater strength than we are, and it multiplies personal resources.

It is faith in oneself though, that sets off this power. It is the heart conviction that regardless of the misfortunes, it is possible to win. I have had my doubts about trying to venture in business and with the change in culture but with the support of my family and the belief in myself, I could sail through. In the following generation, I emphasized the development of this self-confidence at an early age. It is regarding the importance of following your gut feeling, trial and error and

68

going the extra mile. It forms indestructible strength in association with family support.

Family and self-belief maintain cultural harmony with beliefs in our society. Rituals, festivals and common histories are sources of strength as they give us a sense of identity. An example can be my grandchildren who attend family prayer sessions and debates that make them feel confident. The most touching experience came when my granddaughter presented a school project on environmental issues and I could hear how confident she was about it, based on the information she obtained at the family table. It was her faith in herself, and we all gave her support.

Finally, grandchildren make life so much richer, and their presence lifespan enriched with pride and reason. The power of schooling gives the following generation wings in the sky, and a family and a belief in oneself give wings. When I write this autobiography I want my generation to remember these aspects in a way that they will favor them in the future. The real value of life is not in material assets but in the loving, the learning we teach, the strong spirit we foster which is unparalleled by money, etc. With their adoption, the generations that will come to be will not only manage to survive, but to flourish in the knowledge of the direction I would have taken.

69

Chapter 10: Final Thoughts

Legacy and Advice to Future Generations

As I look back at the struggles and dreams in my life, it must feature work, my family, and values. I think towards my legacy and the generations yet to come. At this juncture, where the sun of my years is dipping below the horizon, I find myself enveloped in thoughts of grandchildren, lessons of life and hope for tomorrow. Legacy is not what we collect, but who we love, who we teach wisdom to, and who we inspire to dream.

Grandchildren are in a class of their own, in every society, a grandparent's love is boundless. Grandchildren come first in our lives, not a love of limits where we would do anything for them, and give them everything that we own, and ask for nothing in return. My grandchildren are new iterations of our family story, small drops of sunshine in the most mundane days, warm reminders of the child I was, and the dreams I hope they fulfill in their futures.

One moment that made me incredibly proud happened during a recent family gathering, as we celebrated Diwali. My eldest grandson, only ten years old, spontaneously directed a little skit recounting how our Lord Rama vanquished Ravana.

He not only directed his siblings but also incorporated lessons on respect and persistence that I had shared with him over the years. As I watched his confidence, listening to his words of direction with emphasis, and his teary, hopeful eyes searching the audience for applause, I found immense pride in not just the performance, but the transmission of values in our cultural past that were flourishing in him. I felt that all of my work, in planting seeds of admiration in him, was beginning to bloom into a big flower. At that moment, I was assured that I was fulfilling my role of grandfather to its deepest meaning, not just physically, but through spirits.

The lessons I hope to convey to future generations are deeply rooted in our cultural past. The most important lesson I want to impart to the future generation is to respect their parents. Achieving, may it be wealth, fame, or accomplishments, can never happen without respecting one's own parents. It is the first and most important principle: honor our elders, as they are the ones who design and provide for the existence of your world. Without the notion of respect, no success in the world can ever fill the void you will find yourself in. I do believe that when we respect our parents we are assured of future prosperity and inner peace as always someone else espoused a long time ago.

71

In terms of schooling, my advice is prescribed in two simple, yet deep messages: once again, when you start it do not stop! You must continue to be connected to your schooling with continued connection to your studies. Do not take other interest in the world as interrupts, break or do nothing; but stay focused whatever you are doing.

Looking onwards, my dreams are focused on teaching on-line. Teaching on-line raises the possibilities because it can reach beyond physical boundaries. As a gentleman who always valued education and community, I become excited with the prospect of using online media to provide some value to students with the knowledge I have gained over years. Teaching on-line is a double-edged sword; it is a bridge to modernity, allowing me to connect with learners all over the world. I hope to develop courses that are related to everyday living skills, cultural heritage, and business/community knowledge I have achieved by living in real-time, in agriculture, family businesses, and in the community. As an example, I think of logging into a virtual classroom where I, V.C.Patel explained to youth about ethical business and demonstrating environmentally sustainable farming in extreme climate conditions. This is not about passing on knowledge but creating a worldwide conversation to ensure the completion of reality while considering adapting to technology.

I hope to share reflections of my wise learning using online platforms to students who want to gain knowledge. Over my lifetime, I have been the person who would offer a story to my family throughout gatherings, reminding them of struggles, and endurance along the way whether that be my experiences as a child growing up in Gujarat or later in life with my son doing handyman work abroad. "Growth is about adversity, it is about the soil you are in; nurture it with patience." The eventuality of humanity lies in wisdom; my advice would be rooted in our cultural proverbs and lived experiences.

My greatest legacy would be the lasting impact on my students and family. For my students, I hope to spark an interest in lifelong learning and give them the tools they need to face an unknown future. Imagine if a young entrepreneur started their business and credited my online module with their success, or a student from a remote village engaged with and applied my wisdom about sustainable practices, which improved their community well-being. My impact would move outward affecting a network of empowered people who teach others. This is about planting ideas that last, similar to the way I helped shape the careers of my children.

Another reason for doing this involves my family and how our relationship would strengthen. My grandchildren could join my virtual sessions, see and learn from me in fun and up to date lessons and maybe we even work together on a project on our family history. In too many families, the importance of heritage has diminished over time, while growing pride in our heritage not only benefits our family, but also reinforces a new skill around digital literacy, which has long-term implications for quality of life. Furthermore, my children would be able to witness me creating and seize opportunities using technology, which may inspire them to pursue their own passions, knowing that age does not matter. The emotional result for them would be significant: a grandfather who hasn't just faded into the background but is still carving futures for his family. This would happen through online teaching in any context because our family's lived story isn't frozen in time, it is evolving in tandem with changing times.

In making this happen, there are obstacles such as being familiar with technology tools, developing an audience, and learning how to imagine my life in a digital format. But throughout my life I have chosen continuity as a guiding principle. I'll begin small, perhaps a blog or a few simple videos, and make progress through perseverance. I would also consider platforms such as Coursera and local Indian ed-tech sites to help disseminate my work. In saying this, I want to emphasize that this desire isn't about becoming a 'celebrity' but simply creating value for education and knowledge.

74

In imparting knowledge, I will leave a legacy to students around the world and strengthen my family connections. In the great story of life, this autobiography means that whenever my readers hear of my journey, I will live on in their memory that knowledge and love last forever even when my soul departed from this world.

www.ingramcontent.com/pod-product-compliance
Lightning Source LLC
Chambersburg PA
CBHW051330120626
46547CB00016B/2479